Beachcombers All

Exploring the New England Seashore

Beachcombers All
Exploring the New England Seashore

BY RON ROOD
Illustrated by Reed A. Prescott III

THE NEW ENGLAND PRESS
SHELBURNE, VERMONT

For additional copies of this book or for a catalog of our other
New England and nature titles, please write:

The New England Press
P.O. Box 575
Shelburne, Vermont 05482

ILLUSTRATOR'S ACKNOWLEDGMENTS

I would like to thank the authors and publishers of the following
book for guiding me through this project:

Amos, William H., and Stephen H. Amos. *The Audobon Society Nature
Guide: Atlantic and Gulf Coast.* New York: Alfred A. Knopf, 1985.

In addition I would like to thank David Marsters, Rob Newman,
Peter Straub, and David Thompson. Each went far beyond teaching
their own subject and taught the whole student.

Rood, Ronald N.
    Beachcombers all : exploring the New England seashore / by Ronald Rood ;
illustrated by Reed A. Prescott III.
— 1st ed.
        p.   cm.
    ISBN 0-933050-80-1
    1. Seashore biology—New England. 2. Seashore flora—New
England. 3. Natural history—New England. I. Title.
QH104.5.N4R66 1990
508.14′6′0974—dc20   90-5817
                                                                             CIP

Maps by Kym Pappathanasi

This book is dedicated to the memory of our beloved friend, Freda King. Freda, with her husband Dick, spent many hours with Peg and me along the New England beaches over the years.

I remember as well a huge striped bass—it was too magnificent to keep after I had dragged it up on a wave-washed beach, so I gently let it go again.

So long, old timer.

RONALD ROOD

To my wife Lisa and our explorations at low tide.

REED A. PRESCOTT III

O Lord, how manifold are thy works! in wisdom hast thou made them all: the earth is full of thy riches.

So is this great and wide sea, wherein are things creeping innumerable, both small and great beasts.

There go the ships: there is that leviathan, whom thou hast made to play therein.

PSALMS 104:24-26

Contents

Beachcombers All

Exploring the New England Seashore

CHAPTER 1

Beachcombers All

There's a little of the sea in all of us.

You've heard the crash of breakers against New England's rocks or on its sandy shore, even if only in your imagination. You've heard the scream of the gulls and felt the sting of the salty breeze. They are there and you know it, even if you've yet to experience them for the first time.

The pull of the sea may be a fundamental one indeed. Many scientists believe that life itself began in those sheltering waters. It grew and developed over aeons of time, giving rise to forms that swam and crawled and explored their watery world. Eventually, some primal plant thrust a tentative frond shoreward. Some daring creature quit the shallows for a life on land. Our fascination with the sea may be, in a way, a backward glance at those ancient beginnings.

One singular clue helps give credence to such an idea. This clue is found literally in our blood. Remove the corpuscles and other special substances, and the basic fluid in your veins is amazingly like sea water in its composition. Blood is more diluted, true, but the resemblance between the proportions of many minerals and salts in blood and sea water seems far beyond the vagaries of chance. It's as if, on the journey away from our birthplace, we took with us a souvenir of home.

Whatever the real story is—if, indeed, we can ever know it completely—the spell of the sea remains for many of us. Few people will ever venture upon its broad expanse; fewer still will plunge beneath its depths. But that varied and lively place known as the seashore is within the reach of millions.

Here's something you'll often notice at the seashore. Someone finds a pretty shell, an unusual pebble, a tangle of seaweed tossed up by the waves. Turning it over and examining it, the sharp-eyed explorer shows it to the next person who comes along. These two are then joined by somebody else—and soon there's a little knot of people, chattering and exclaiming over a bit of debris. Strangers all, but friends for a moment together—where but at the beach?

That's what we can accomplish, perhaps, with this book. Friends in discovery, we can stroll among the dunes and along the beaches of New England, you and I, or scramble over wave-worn rocks. Along the way we may find a beach plum or a sea cucumber—the one a plant, the other an animal. And if the ship-worm that tunneled through that driftwood isn't a worm, what is it?

We'll discover how the lowly starfish single-handedly opens an oyster, while people must resort to a hammer or other tool for the same purpose. We can contemplate a flock of sanderlings as these little birds advance and retreat, advance and retreat—following one wave after another for their daily food.

Yes, the beach is its own special world, a world to add a zest for discovery and a balm for the distracted soul. To walk along that shore, picking up a broken clamshell here and overturning a castaway plank there, is to shed a hundred troubles. And if you let the beachcomber in you have its way, you may well carry home a weathered souvenir that will take you back to that very beach—at least in your memory—for years to come.

CHAPTER 2

The Dunes and Beyond

You may walk across the seashore, in a way, before you ever get there. The sea is so restless and changing that today's shoreline is sometimes tomorrow's sand dunes and produces the next decade's shrubbery.

At the turn of the century, for instance, a certain navigation structure in Virginia was at the edge of the waves. Now it's three miles inland and surrounded by pine trees. It's the Chincoteague lighthouse on the island of Assateague—a good example of how the seacoast varies over the years. You may find evidence of such change along almost any shore.

A stroll toward the ocean often leads one across brush and weeds and little trees that shelter animal populations. These little communities are the result of the process of succession, as it's called. At various points in the transition from beach to brushland, one species after another appears like an actor on a stage. Each is there for just a while, then something takes its place.

For now, let's walk along the dunes and look at the plants we find there. One shrub that thrives in the raw, windy, salty air is the sturdy shiny-leaved, waxy-fruited bayberry. Wax from its whitish, buckshot-size berries has been used for generations in the making of candles. (The wax can be extracted by boiling the berries in water.)

BAYBERRY

Bayberry is a sun-loving plant and must give way when trees move in to shade the soil. Until then this bushy plant, sometimes as tall as a person, is a most typical New England dune dweller.

First cousin of the bayberry is the sweet "fern," so called because of its aromatic, fernlike foliage. One or two feet high, this little shrub has a small burrlike fruit and does fine in dry, sunny, sandy areas. So does a true fern—the brake, or bracken, whose woody stem divides into three frond-bearing branches.

Sweet fern leaflets, by the way, add a nice scent when enclosed in a letter. I often suggest this when I take kids at camp on nature walks. They dutifully write a letter home. (Often, it's the only letter the parents get from them all summer.)

Much loved, and seldom higher than your head, is a shrub with attractive white blossoms and tasty little yellow-to-purple fruit: the beach plum. Its scraggly gray stems with their finely saw-toothed oval leaves are familiar behind beaches or dunes from New Brunswick to Virginia. Beach plums have given their name to Plum Island, near Ipswich, Massachusetts.

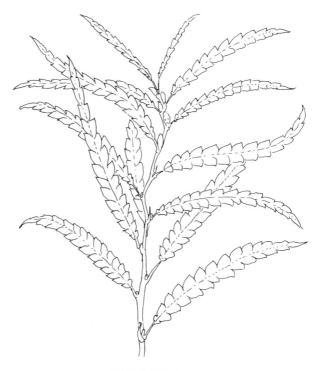

SWEET FERN

BRACKEN FERN

5

BEECH PLUM

Some of the best beach plum jelly we've ever tasted was on the breakfast table at a little restaurant in Rhode Island. The fruit also makes a delicious jam. Be sure the pits are removed, however, or you may remember that first bite for a long time.

Foxes, raccoons, squirrels, mice, and chipmunks feast on beach plums. So do many species of birds. Sometimes, when dead-ripe plums begin to ferment, you'll see an interesting performance: tipsy robins, thrushes, and other birds drowsily enjoying their version of Happy Hour in the late summer sun.

Much of the sandy soil of the dunes is held together by one of the shore's most important plants: American beach grass. With tough, slender leaves, leathery stems, and an underground maze of connecting roots, this grass is a vital stabilizer for the blowing sand.

Not only does beach grass hold those crystalline particles together; it rises to meet almost any challenge. During a drought, the leaves roll into a tube to conserve moisture. The force of a gale may bury it in a wall of sand, but this undaunted plant is a true survivor. It quickly grows several inches—or even several feet—until it is on top once more.

Adventitious roots soon spring out along the buried stem of beach grass as it struggles upward. These roots secure the drifted sand as it builds. Sometimes the whole affair grows as high as a house. A massive dune is stabilized by the network of hidden roots and surmounted by the waving grass blades of a plant that seems to be only two or three feet high.

You can see mile after mile of this irrepressible grass at work on the Cape Cod National Seashore. Indeed, you'll see it on the dunes just behind almost any sandy beach along America's entire East Coast. Sometimes, where the march of the wind-driven dunes has been more sedate, you'll find many other seaside plants poking bravely above the choking sand as well. Their little tips may be all that is visible of weeds, shrubs, branches—and even entire trees—that have been engulfed over the years.

Seldom does any plant form a natural, pure stand with no other species for neighbors, and beach grass is no exception. Tendrils of the beach pea twine among the grass blades, helping to raise the pea's attractive pink or blue flowers up to the sun. You may

BEACH PEA

DUSTY MILLER

find the dusty miller, a plant whose divided leaves are densely covered with the little whitish hairs that give it its name. If you pad along with bare feet, you may also discover all you care to know about cockleburs.

The sand and pebbles of these dune areas are used as nesting places by some shorebirds. The eggs of plovers, sandpipers, gulls, and terns are camouflaged to match the color of the sand. So are their hatchlings, who are so cleverly speckled they're almost impossible to see. Little plovers and sandpipers are precocious youngsters, leaving their shallow pebble-and-sand nests soon after they hatch.

Other shorebirds raise their young far north of our New England area, and we see most of them only during the spring and fall migrations. Their habit of nesting in the remote northland is fortunate indeed, considering the thousands of human visitors who romp along the shore. At Maine's Popham Beach, for instance, it has been necessary to put a fence around several acres of sun-warmed sand where the rare piping plover and the least tern lay their eggs.

Birds and other animals are often responsible for the presence of several edible plants in the dunes. Wild grape, bittersweet, wild cherry, sumac, wild rose, blueberry, and even poison ivy have hard seeds that pass through birds' digestive tracts virtually unharmed. "Planted" here and there in the musky droppings, they're a record of the visits of wildlife species—and an invitation to more of the same.

PIPING PLOVER

POISON IVY

Cottontail rabbits dash through the shrubbery and grasses in the dunes. They nibble at the greenery—even prickly rose and blackberry bushes—leaving a distinctive slanted cut, the trademark of those buck teeth. Mice of several species gather grass seeds, wild fruits, and cherry pits. Shrews prowl along on their endless hunt for any appropriate food, from beetles and grasshoppers to bird eggs and mice—even mice that are twice the size of their feisty little captors.

The shrews themselves may fall prey to skunks, raccoons, and opossums. Those creatures are inveterate scroungers, seeking candidates for their anything-goes appetites: grubs, snails, frogs, snakes, and the eggs and young of birds. Skunks amble along the ground, digging for grubs and earthworms, while 'coons and 'possums often climb trees and bushes and man-made objects. In the process they leave no stone—or garbage pail—unturned.

OPOSSUM

AMERICAN KESTREL

Many creatures who live behind the dunes do so because it's a transition zone, showing what is often called the "edge effect." You can see this effect at the border of a field or in a large opening in a forest. Not only are there edibles of many kinds here, but protective cover is near at hand. So living creatures are provided with two basic needs: food and shelter.

My wife, Peg, and I have gone on all-day bird walks along these areas on many occasions. A day when we don't see several dozen species of birds is a rare one indeed. The best tally we ever had was with eight other people at the Cape Cod National Seashore: we saw exactly 120 species between dawn and dusk.

To name a few outstanding birds, we'd have to include the American kestrel, a little falcon about the size of a robin. With reddish tail and back, it has a habit of perching on wires or dead tree limbs. Two dark vertical stripes on its face plus sparrow streaking on its body help distinguish it from the plain-colored mourning dove—a slightly larger bird that also perches in open places. You'll often seen the mourning dove on the ground at the edge of a road or pathway; it flies up with a whistling sound, showing the white sides of its pointed tail.

MOURNING DOVE

A common bird of prey, larger than a crow, flies over these grassy areas: the marsh hawk, or northern harrier. It drifts just a few feet above the ground, holding its wings in a shallow V as it searches for rodents and grasshoppers. The white patch just ahead of its tail is a diagnostic mark. Male marsh hawks are grayer than the brownish females.

Woodpeckers drill into the scraggly trees and inspect driftwood that's been abandoned by the sea. Their activities suggest they're attacking the wood, but they're actually excavating for borers and other insects. One time, when we saw fresh chips below a longitudinal hole made by a pileated woodpecker, we asked the householder if the bird had been around lately. "He was here yesterday," she said. Then she added significantly, "But we took care of him."

You may see a flycatcher at work among the insects, catching them in the air with an audible snap of its beak. The various species of flycatcher, all grayish in color, are usually hard to tell apart. None is very musical, but one kind, the eastern phoebe, "keeps saying its name," as my mother informed me: an unmusical, emphatic *fee*-be. The phoebe also frequently pumps its tail while it perches.

Swallows of several kinds are constantly on the wing during daylight. Among the world's best aerialists, they may fly just above the ground for a moment, then zoom skyward or sideways in almost any direction. Each of these dizzying gymnastic feats probably means there's one less mosquito or gnat or greenhead fly to visit your unprotected epidermis.

Less spectacular in flight but familiar to nearly everyone who visits areas near the water are the grackles and meadowlarks, as well as the flocks of blackbirds. The colorful shoulder patch of the redwing blackbird is distinctive. The meadowlark, with the black V crossing its yellow underside, has a high, drawn-out whistled note. Grackles boast long tails, croaky voices, and the unsettling habit of pilfering the eggs and young of other birds when the parents aren't around.

The varied communities in areas above the beach, from straggly trees and bushes to open sand, present many opportunities for insect life. Butterflies catch the sunlight as they visit flowers along the way. Sometimes in the fall, black and orange migrating monarch butterflies may descend on the bushes—or even on a single bush—by the dozens. Yellow sulphurs, small orange-

EASTERN PHOEBE

MEADOWLARK

brown skippers, metallic little blues—these and other butterflies scatter spots of color as they dance over the dunes.

Dragonflies and damselflies cut their swaths through the gnat and mosquito populations. Often, when dragonflies catch an insect in the basket formed by their legs, they consume it as they travel, like a youngster walking down the street with a candy bar. Damselflies, who have a more fluttery flight, usually take their unfortunate prey to a nearby perch, where they dine on it at their leisure.

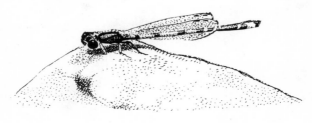

DAMSELFLY

14

Ants build their homes among the grass roots and under chunks of debris. Sometimes they fall prey to that patient digger, the ant lion. This squat little creature, about a quarter inch long, makes a cone-shaped pit in the soft sand. You can find the ant lion's dimplelike depressions, about half an inch deep, in the driest, sandiest areas. Hidden at the bottom of each is the spraddle-legged occupant. As the victim struggles to climb out of the pit, sand rolls down beneath its feet—and the ant lion helps the process by tossing sand grains that shower back down on the captive.

Another insect predator is the colorful tiger beetle. Decked in iridescent greens, blues, reds, or even stripes, this creature is a little larger than a raisin. Astonishingly swift of foot, the tiger beetle half-races, half-flies to catch moths, damselflies, and other insects. It has even been known to leap into the air after a passing fly.

TIGER BEETLE

The uneven ground between dunes may form hollows that hold rainwater or the offerings of a little brook. Muskrats come across such freshwater ponds in their travels, as do water birds, aquatic insects, and even fish. Once I watched a great blue heron land at such a pond, disgorge a groggy but still-living fish, stab halfheartedly at it, and fly away. From antics such as this, bodies of water sometimes get their finny residents. Fish may also colonize new ponds when their sticky eggs hitch a ride on water birds.

Other herons, sandpipers, ducks, and even geese visit these little ponds. Snapping turtles, painted turtles, and the eastern

PAINTED TURTLE

water snake wander and discover potential new homes as well. Garter snakes, while not aquatic, may settle close by in response to the presence of frogs and toads near the water's edge if the water is fresh. Salt water is deadly to frogs and toads—indeed, to the whole amphibian tribe.

One more resident of this region is very much a part of the sea-coast scene: the bipedal, noisy, often wasteful, but sometimes deeply appreciative human being. Traditionally, the shoreline itself has been for the use of all, but personal access to it may not be so easy anymore. In many places everything above high-tide line has been paved over, built over, lawned over, or swimming-pooled over.

Luckily, the establishment of state and municipal parks has saved many miles of shoreline for general use. But these, too, are being squeezed now, as more people flock to the beaches. So if you are thinking of heading for the shore, you'd better do it soon.

Even this book, based as it is on years of beachcombing and sand-trotting and rock-hopping, may be of little value if you cannot get to the beach, despite the feeling of my enthusiastic friend, the late Bill Wessel. Bill felt that "any sign telling you to 'keep out' really means 'welcome.' "

Maybe. But not always.

CHAPTER 3

Tidal Marshes and Mud Flats

One thing is certain about tidal marshes and mud flats: they aren't flat.

Not if you look at them closely, that is. They're pockmarked by tiny craters, crisscrossed by mazes of lines, eroded with gullies, and bumpy with hills and valleys that'd challenge a mountain climber if they were a few thousand times bigger.

As we've been told for years, these broad deltas and river mouths—flooded by the incoming tide and abandoned as the water retreats—are the nurseries for many kinds of seashore life. It's hard to realize this, however, when you stand at the edge of a wetland area or if you slog through its gluey mud, smell the sulfurous odor of decaying plants and animals, and listen to the little ticking noises as the water level changes and bubbles of gas come to the surface. This smelly place—the cradle of life?

Yes, indeed. With a bucket, binoculars, and a magnifying glass—plus plenty of fortitude—you'd be able to see it for yourself. There are members of almost every family of animal life in a tidal marsh or mud flat. If you dare, put on a pair of boots, or well-laced old shoes (not sandals or slip-ons; you'll walk right out of them in the clinging ooze), and make their acquaintance at low tide.

The plants that grow here can be of several kinds. Most common is the tough, slender cordgrass. Cordgrass is vital to the stability of a tidal marsh; its sturdy rootstocks thread their way among the soil and silt, binding everything together in a fibrous mat that's almost immune to wind and wave. The leaves of cordgrass curl into a tubelike, almost indestructible cord when dry; hence the name. They can be woven into baskets and mats.

Cordgrass has round stems, as does the tall (eight to twelve feet high) plume grass or marsh reed—also called phragmites. Both cordgrass and plume grass have fruiting heads at the tips of their stems. Seaside rushes, which often grow in the same area, have their seedlike fruits below the tip. Rushes and their cousins, the sedges, have triangular stems.

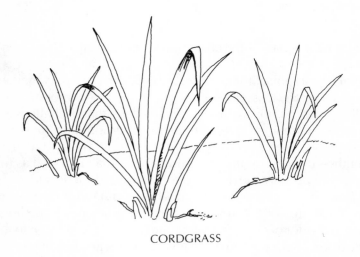

CORDGRASS

A whole patch of cordgrass or of tall, waving plume grass may really be all one plant. The hidden runners of the parent give rise to shoots that become new offspring; these produce more of the same until an entire tidal marsh is populated by thousands of stems, all connected. There are many of these marshy patches along U.S. Routes 1 and 1A, especially on the Rhode Island coast.

The attractive sea lavender grows in these salty areas. It has simple, elongated, leathery leaves at the base of a foot-high flower stem. In summer, this stem, branching at its upper end, bears small flowers in rows along its side branches. Sea lavender is often used in dried-flower arrangements.

Among the many other common flowering plants is the seashore goldenrod, with conspicuous clusters of yellow flowers in late summer. There are also two wild cousins of the common hollyhock. One of these is the tall rose mallow, with large four-inch pink or white five-petaled flowers and pointed (sometimes lobed) oval leaves, woolly beneath, on a head-high stalk. The other species is the attractive little marsh mallow, two or three

SEA LAVENDER

MARSH MALLOW

ROSE MALLOW

SEASHORE GOLDENROD

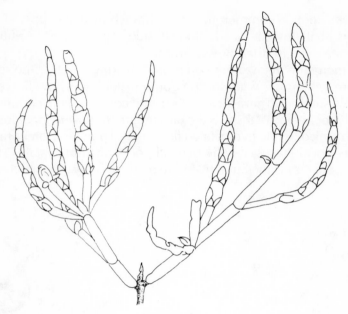

GLASSWORT

feet high, with smaller (one-inch) pink blooms in clusters, plus three-lobed leaves. Its roots have been used in—you guessed it—marshmallows.

One peculiar plant looks like a thick, translucent, six-inch moss: the samphire, or glasswort. Its succulent, leafless stems are tender and salty to the taste; hence its scientific name *Salicornia*—"the salty plant shaped like a little horn."

In the wet mud you may see a maze of trails left by thousands of the eighth-inch-long crustaceans known as isopods. Other trails are made by saltwater cousins of the earthworm as they explore for food, wandering about or making radiating lines from a central burrow. Like many denizens of the tidal marshes, they are not fussy; if something might be edible, down it goes.

Some marine snails climb up on the marsh grass to await the return of the water with the tide. Others plow a zigzag trail through the mud. Clams and mussels leave no trail at all.

Soft-shell or steamer clams are buried a few inches deep; their long siphons poke up to the surface. Quahogs, or hard-shells (called cherrystones when small) are in more sandy areas. Smooth blue mussels remain attached by threads to an old shell, a waterlogged piece of driftwood, or to each other. Gray-ribbed mussels make their home half buried in the soil at the high-tide level.

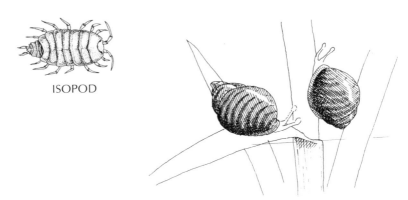

ISOPOD

PERIWINKLES ON GRASS

QUAHOG

STEAMER CLAM

BLUE MUSSEL

GRAY-RIBBED MUSSEL

21

As water flows onto the flats and out again, it often leaves pools on the surface. In these pools you'll find glass shrimps, their bodies so transparent you can see the beating of their hearts and the workings of their innards. Crabs of several species may be here, too, buried up to the eyes in the mud.

One of the most personable of these crustaceans is the fiddler crab. During low tide, the fiddler crab burrows into the mud near the high-tide mark, making holes from the size of a pencil to that of a quarter. As it runs about between tides, it seeks bits of seaweed and other algae, and an occasional worm for variety. Scare the fiddler and it scurries for its hole; then it elbows its way partly out again to see if the coast is clear.

FIDDLER CRAB

The mature fiddler's body is almost an inch in size. The male has one giant pincher much larger than the other; it waves this claw back and forth as if playing a violin—hence its name. This action apparently serves as a warning to other males and a come-on to females.

When the water rises, the fiddlers retire to their burrows, and they come out again at low tide. They'll follow this cycle for days, even if they are moved to a moist terrarium many miles from the sea. Apparently the rhythm of the tidal marsh remains deep in their small crab-consciousness.

The colorful—and highly edible and feisty—blue crab lives in these marshy waters. This talented swimmer's blue, red, and olive colors are attractive indeed, as it prowls among the shallows.

If the sunlight slants at the proper angle, you'll see that the shallow water is teeming with thousands of floating creatures. Under a magnifying glass, these become exquisite jewels. Tiny plants, called diatoms, look like miniature discs, triangles, cubes, and assorted other shapes. Microscopic animals have ruby-red eyes or iridescent bodies or fire-orange sides, while others are colorless. There are fat ones, skinny ones, many-legged ones, and fuzzy ones. All of these are kinds of plankton, the floating life that is the "grass" of this shallow tidal pasture. Feasting on this abundant repast may be little fishes of many species—safe for a while from their larger cousins until the tide returns. Later, when they've grown bigger, many will venture out into the ocean.

The rising tidal waters may transport floating plants and animals to the land and then abandon them there. Seaweeds of several kinds, whole schools of fish, an occasional squid, sponges, and fish eggs may be so stranded. On one Rhode Island tidal flat, I once saw scores of red jellyfish, each about the dimensions of a soup plate, lying helplessly on the mud. They pulsated weakly but were going nowhere. Soon they'd dry to cardboard-thin discs of death and become food for new legions of life.

In some places as you walk along the mud flat, you may see a leathery cylinder the size of your finger poking a couple of inches above the mud. This is the tunnel of the tube worm, a marine relative of the common earthworm. There are several kinds of these creatures. Some remain well concealed, taking in water and straining their food from it. Others extend feathery tentacles like a plume, occasionally closing up and feeding on whatever their living net has provided.

A number of worms are more direct in their eating habits. The two nipping jaws of the eight-inch clamworm attack soft-bodied snails, clams, and even its own cousins. The slightly smaller bloodworms have four little hooks that accomplish the same purpose. Both creatures are red (large clamworms are often an iridescent coppery-green), with many fleshy bristles on their sides. Another relative, the scaleworm, has tough plates like a tiny seagoing armadillo.

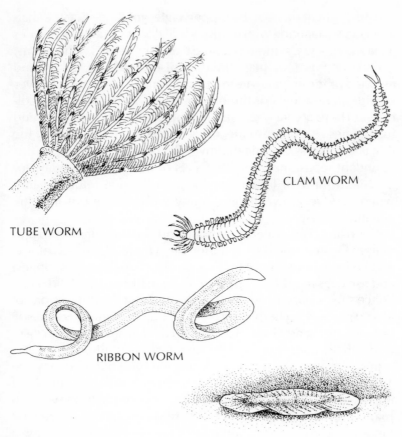

TUBE WORM

CLAM WORM

RIBBON WORM

(not drawn to scale)

SPECKLED FLATWORM

Dig through the mud, and you'll probably encounter other elongated creatures. They're often categorized as worms, but they may actually be related to each other no more closely than a goldfish is to a starfish. One of the largest is the ribbon worm, or nemertine, half an inch wide and sometimes as much as four feet long. It's white or pink—quite an unexpected color to see in the black ooze. There's also an oval, spotted worm about the size of a quarter: the speckled flatworm. It crawls, somewhat like a snail, or it swims gracefully, like a flag rippling in the breeze.

The hundreds of species of marine roundworms or nematodes are mostly tiny and hard to tell apart without a microscope. But their importance is enormous: they swim about freely, crawl along, or live in the tissues of clams, fish, water weeds—and for that matter, in the tissues of the people who look at them. So abundant are roundworms that, if everything in a marshy mud flat could be removed except these little creatures, scientists say, we'd still be able to see a ghostly image of the whole marsh—soil, plants, animals and all—outlined in roundworms.

All this burgeoning life is stirred up and mixed together by those daily tides. Much of it is then transported to the complex food net in the sea itself, but a good portion remains behind as the staff of life for the birds, mammals, and other vertebrates who spend part of their existence here.

Muskrats feed on reeds and rushes that grow where a stream flows into the mudflat, lessening the salinity of the water. Snapping turtles poke along in these waters, on the lookout for a bit of carrion, an unwary fish, or—if the snapper is big and tough—a prowling raccoon or incautious muskrat. A friend of ours once

MUSKRAT

witnessed a battle between a snapper and an otter. It was an evenly matched contest. But the turtle's bulldog grip won the battle when the rising tide came in: turtles can hold their breath under water much longer than otters can.

Many tidal marshes are vital staging areas where shorebirds fuel up for their long migrations. Sandpipers may arrive by the thousands in late summer from their nesting grounds in the far north. Brownish in color, they run about on the sand and mud, probing in staccato thrusts of the beak for mollusks, worms, and crustaceans. Back again the next spring, they feed and rest on their way in the other direction.

The great blue heron, one of the wariest of birds despite its yard-high stance and wingspan of nearly six feet, waits like a statue in the shallows for fish. Ducks and geese tip up as they sozzle through the mud for worms, snails, and the tender parts of plants. An osprey hovers above on beating wings for a

OSPREY

moment, then plummets down to get a fish. The roughened scales on its feet are perfect tongs to hold the slippery, struggling meal.

Sparrows, warblers, blackbirds, and other vocalists keep the tidal marsh lively with their songs, their squabbles over territory, and their constant searches for food. In autumn, after these birds depart, the place seems shockingly quiet. All that's heard is the gentle ticking of the air bubbles and the whisper of the tide as it retreats—only to advance once again like a probing stream of lava around little mounds and into unnoticed valleys in the mud.

Thus, as it has for millions of years, the cradle of seashore life faithfully and quietly continues to rock.

CHAPTER 4

Stern and Rockbound

Few coastlines are more dramatic than the rugged parts of our New England coastline. There, staunch and solid, great boulders and cliffs are the first unyielding objects encountered by waves driven from storms at sea. Breakers hurl themselves at the craggy bulwarks again and again, sending spray high into the air.

Even in calmer times such shores are fascinating. Oceanic swells surge among rocks and ledges, gurgling and murmuring, and tons of water flood over boulders and through wave-worn channels. Then a moment's pause, and with a sigh the juggernaut retreats—to gather for another attack.

Some of the most spectacular New England shores are found along the coast of Maine. At Acadia National Park at Bar Harbor, for instance, you can contemplate the pinkish-white granite ledges and the massive dikes or "streams" of dark basalt poking up through them. And streams they once were, when the molten black substance pushed up and flowed like thick syrup through the granite that lay over it.

Those once-rugged masses are pavement-smooth now. Polished by wind and water, they cover acres of Acadia's shoreline. Waves crash against their edges, foaming and boiling. At the famous Thunder Hole the sea crowds into a narrow cleft in the rock and compresses the air ahead of it until the pressure explodes with a booming *huff!*—shooting a misty fountain as much as a hundred feet into the air, especially after a storm.

The hundreds of islands and rocky spits on the coastline were once the tops of hills and ridges, according to geologists. You can see this, sometimes, when the retreating tide exposes the valleys between them. Such a coastline results from a slow sinking of the land—only an inch or two per century, perhaps, but the sea has plenty of time.

This nubbly terrain extends southward from Maine. In its outcrops here and there along New England's oceanic frontier, its boulders are scattered, alternating with sandy beaches. Along the way are the rocky Isles of Shoals, off Portsmouth, New Hampshire, plus dozens of islands, of which Nantucket and Martha's Vineyard are the largest. There are also crags with names like Stony Point, Rocky Neck, Shipwreck, and Ocean Bluff. As one disgruntled Yankee dryly remarked, "They say the first Pilgrims landed on a rock. What else could they land on?"

Often the contours of wave-worn crags are hidden beneath a mantle of rockweed. Little gas-filled bladders on their fronds give buoyancy to these branching algae when the water covers them.

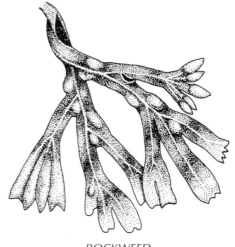

ROCKWEED

As the tide retreats, the weeds collapse into an olive-colored mat that may be more than a foot thick.

Turn aside a swatch of these rubbery plants, and you'll find a quiet world waiting for the return of the tide. You'll see many other algae: crinkly green sea lettuce, for instance, plus feather-weed, along with spongy green-black Codium and reddish Irish "moss." There are little sponges, too—some the shape and color of a crust of bread and some descriptively termed "dead man's fingers."

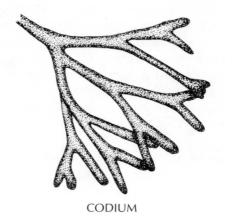

CODIUM

Little rock eels wriggle through this underwater forest. Gray periwinkle snails the size of a marble browse on plant materials and debris. Pointed-shelled whelks, or drills, creep along on a more sinister mission: to find a clam or mussel and pierce its shell with their rasping, tonguelike radula. Then they dine on their hapless prey. You often see shells with these little round holes washed up on the beach.

But the mussels hold their own abundantly. Steely blue-black, thousands of these bivalves ("two shells") attach themselves to rocks, to wooden piers, to almost anything—including each other—by tough filaments known as byssal threads. From there, they filter small floating organisms out of the water. Sometimes they feed so well, they grown from pinhead size to more than two inches in a single year.

Marine annelids—cousins of the earthworm—creep among the thousands of close-packed mussels. So do many-hued sea slugs, whose branching gills resemble a coat of feathers. There are rock crabs with shells ranging from solid green to patchy camouflage colors, plus slender hydroids that look like underwater twigs and branches.

The hydroids are cousins of the corals, jellyfish, and sea anemones. Most corals inhabit warmer seas, while jellyfish swim in open water, opening and closing like umbrellas. Sea anemones collapse to shapeless blobs on the rocks between the tides, but they regain their exquisite flowery form when the water returns. There they wait for an unwary fish to touch their innocent-looking "petals." Their paralyzing sting, luckily, has little or no effect on your bare hands or feet.

In the subtidal waters, below the lowest ebb of the tide, you may see green sea urchins, looking like thorny golf balls, scraping algae off the rocks. Their distant cousins, the starfish, wander along in search of a mussel or clam. When a starfish finds one

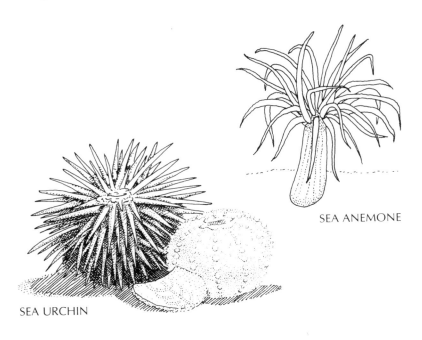

SEA ANEMONE

SEA URCHIN

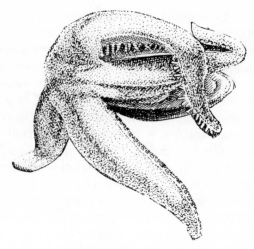

STARFISH OPENING A CLAM

of these bivalves, it wraps it in a deadly embrace. The starfish pulls inexorably at the mollusk's shells with hundreds of tiny sucking tube feet along its five arms. The weary mollusk finally collapses, and its shells gape open. Everting its stomach (that is, turning it inside out), the starfish envelops the body of its victim, digests it in place, retracts its stomach, and gently glides away.

Rocky clefts may also shelter the oddball sea cucumber, another starfish relative. Greenish-black and shaped like its garden namesake, the sea cucumber extends a bushy mass of mucus-covered tentacles. Drifting organisms get tangled in the mucus and end up as food when their captor sticks the tentacles in its mouth. It licks them off, mucus and all, the way you might taste jam with your finger if you don't have a spoon.

Limpets—little mollusks shaped like a shallow inverted cone or hat—cling to the rocks. The size of a coin, the limpet leaves its chosen spot to graze on nearby algae when the tide is full. When the water retreats, it returns home like a little cow coming back to the barn.

The animals that are most abundant on the rocks often seem not to be living at all. These are the white, limy-shelled crustaceans known as barnacles. Distant relatives of the crab and the lobster, barnacles attach themselves to solid objects with a special glue. Dentists and engineers have long tried to imitate this glue, for an adhesive that sticks to a wet surface would be valuable indeed. So far, however, the secret has remained with the barnacle.

The barnacle extends its feathery legs out into the water, then quickly curls them back between the shells and to its mouth, several dozen times a minute. This catch-as-catch-can method of scooping a meal with an active little throw net attests to the abundance of food in the ocean. Rocks and ledges may be encrusted with millions of barnacles.

Occasionally you'll see a bed of oysters, also wet-cemented to the rocks. They feed on bits of plankton, the tiny floating plants and animals that are also consumed by barnacles and mussels.

SEA CUCUMBER

BARNACLES
(not drawn to scale)

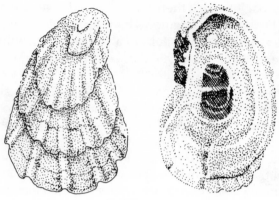

OYSTER SHELLS

When young, oysters swim freely through the water, but they soon settle down on rocks, on pilings, or on other oysters. Then they develop limy little shells. Oysters prefer somewhat brackish conditions, so look for them near the mouths of streams or other freshwater sources. This helps account for their abundance in Chesapeake Bay, where the Potomac River mingles with the sea.

In some places the boulders have shattered into smaller cobbles and pebbles. Worn into a round shape by the ceaseless waves, they clatter as they roll up the beach and back. Few plants or animals can live on such an active surface, but the watery soil beneath abounds with life.

Human generations have long enjoyed the natural charm of these cobble beaches, many of which are found in Maine. Now, however, less benign visitors are gnawing away where great storms have done little more than rearrange the shoreline. These intruders are machines that scoop up the cobbles, for use in modern versions of the old cobblestone street. In national parks are admonitions to "leave nothing but a footprint; take nothing but a picture," but no such protection is afforded most cobble beaches. Many of them have vanished already, so if you'd like to see one, you may have to look quick.

An occasional sandpiper inspects the rocks for worms or crustaceans. Ruddy turnstones, looking like chestnut-backed robins in a clown mask, find their food by flipping aside shells and pebbles, as their name suggests. Gulls bring crabs and choice garbage to the rocks, where they hammer their treasures into bite-sized bits.

Double-crested cormorants, dark in color, fly singly or in long lines above the water. After landing and swimming a moment, they do an arching surface dive as they plunge down for fish. In Asia, these birds may be tethered to a long line tied about their necks. Seizing a fish, the cormorant cannot swallow it past the line. Choking and gasping, the bird is hauled in, relieved of its catch—and tossed out to do it again.

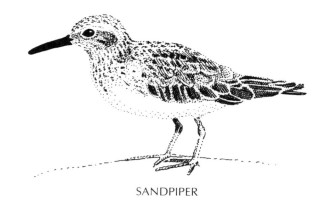

SANDPIPER

RUDDY TURNSTONE

Flotillas, or "rafts," of sea ducks often feed just offshore. They may appear in great numbers or in flocks of a dozen or less. Those with bodies all dark except for small patches of white on the head are probably surf scoters. White-winged scoters also have a small wing marking. The common eider has a long sloping beak profile, plus conspicuous white sides on the males, while the brown females show marked bars on the back.

One distinctive sea bird, the Atlantic puffin, is far better known than its actual numbers would merit. The puffin looks somewhat like a little black-suited duck in a clown mask. It's native to our offshore rocky islands, but few such places now provide the puffin with the shelter it needs. Predatory gulls and the pressure

ATLANTIC PUFFIN

of civilization have forced it from all but the remotest islands. There, beneath a rocky shelf or in a burrow made by the male, the embattled bird hides its single egg.

Attempts to help the puffin reestablish itself have had some encouraging results. At present, however, there are far more puffin photographs, note cards, and refrigerator magnets than there are puffins in real life.

Rarely, a harbor seal drifts by just offshore. As its rounded head breaks the surface, you may be startled and think some daredevil human is swimming near the rocks. On other occasions you might glimpse half a dozen of these spotted gray mammals sunbathing on a ledge just above the water.

Except for a few birds and mammals, however, nearly all the activity of a rocky shore takes place virtually unseen. It's a ballet of sorts, performed back and forth with each wave. Standing near it you might think it just a noisy, boisterous place where the water crashes, the rocks stand firm, and nothing else happens.

A closer look, however, shows that it is more than that—much more. And yet we've only skimmed the surface.

CHAPTER 5

The Sandy Shore

Boisterous as the ocean may be when it smashes against a rocky shore, there's at least a solid base for living things to attach themselves if they can just hang on. A sandy beach seldom yields even that much stability, however. Every wave spreads a layer of sand as the water tumbles forward, then drags it back again.

Indeed, the whole beach may be on a precarious footing. It can be hard to predict just where a sandy shore ends and the dunes of Chapter 2 begin. A dune area—really a dried out beach—can revert to its old ways after a storm, and the same violent weather may cause the sea to abandon one beach even as it forms another. Hence some of the plants and animals of this chapter can also be found in the dunes, and vice versa.

The shifting world of wave-washed sand requires that its inhabitants have special means of survival. Some cling to almost anything that offers a bit of support. A chunk of wood, for instance, becomes an impromptu little life raft, bumping along with dozens of passengers—all of whom are tough enough or resilient enough to withstand the ride.

Such passengers might include slipper shells, which look somewhat like their namesakes, often stacked on top of each other. There may also be encrusting sponges, fuzzy mats of bry-

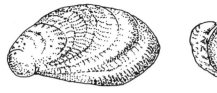
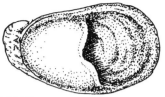

SLIPPER SHELLS

ozoans or moss animals, plus mussels and oysters. Often this little wooden raft is riddled like a piece of Swiss cheese with the tunnels of crustaceans known as gribbles, plus the wood-boring clams called shipworms.

Some creatures merely go with the flow, so to speak, of the waves. Small fish—often the young of larger species—feed on the microscopic organisms drifting about them. If you look at the right moment, you can occasionally see these fish in the transparent greenish curl of an incoming breaker just before it tumbles into foam. The little fish retreat to deeper, safer water at the last moment.

One sand-dweller whose existence depends on the wash of the waves is the hippa, or mole crab. With its tail tucked under its cylindrical body and its legs pulled close to its sides, the hippa

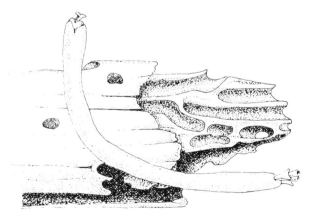

SHIPWORM

39

has the size and general contour of an olive. It tumbles along with a foaming breaker, then anchors itself in the sand when the water goes slack. With feathery antennae spread like a net, the hippa catches plankton and other floating organisms that rush past in the retreating flood.

Little side-swimmers, sometimes dubbed sand fleas, live by the thousands in debris tossed up by the tide. They feed on bits of plant and animal material. They're not really fleas at all, but amphipod crustaceans—distant relatives of shrimps and of the familiar little pill "bugs" and sow "bugs" that live under logs and stones on land.

One creature that can often be seen just below the line of breakers is the attractive lady crab. This "calico crab," as it's also called, is light in color and dotted with scores of tiny red freckles. An accomplished swimmer when necessary to escape a sudden change in the undertow, the calico crab nearly buries itself in the bottom sand. Hidden thus in the shallows, its two dark, stalked eyes poke out and its claws are poised as it waits for a passing fish, a sea worm, or even a set of unprotected toes. It quickly darts away from the toes, but—as I've discovered many times—stepping on it can be a memorable experience.

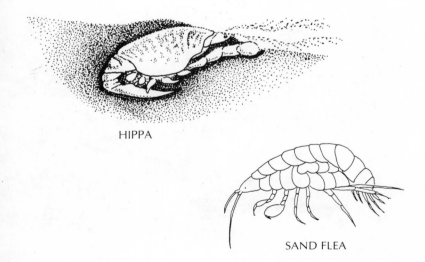

HIPPA

SAND FLEA

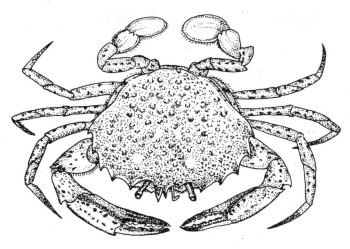

LADY CRAB

Picking its way slowly over the bottom is the spider crab, a mud-colored, ungainly-looking creature. The leg span of New England specimens seldom would stretch across a dinner plate, although the outstretched arms of the North Pacific king crab, their relative, occasionally reach ten feet across. This latter crab supplies the large red and white crab legs in the fish market. Since spider crabs cannot swim, anglers often put a small cork just above the fishhook to float the bait a few inches out of the inquisitive scavenger's reach.

One of the most familiar "crabs" is not a crab at all: the bizarre creature known as the horseshoe crab. Shaped somewhat like an upside-down soup plate and hinged near the middle, this species has been peacefully plowing its way along ocean bottoms virtually unchanged since before the days of the dinosaurs. It is truly a living fossil.

The horseshoe crab uses its ten legs for walking, swimming, and picking up small mollusks and worms. The wicked-looking tail spike would be a dangerous weapon, I suppose, but its main use seems to be to help its owner right itself when upset. If it is threatened, the horseshoe crab simply hunkers down into the

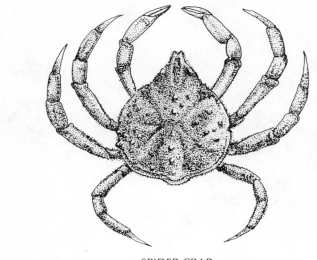

SPIDER CRAB

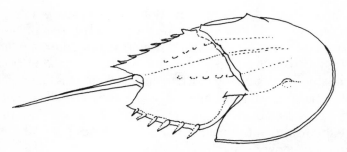

HORSESHOE CRAB

sand, and it's about as easy to dislodge as—well, as an inverted soup plate.

In late May or early June horseshoe crabs come ashore by the thousands. First to leave the waves are the females, about to deposit their eggs. Clinging to each female, one behind the other, may be a train of as many as half a dozen males. She lays the eggs in the sand at high-tide mark; the first male scatters sperm over them. So do the other males, in what must be a "me too" kind of performance. Then the whole procession heads back to sea.

Gulls sometimes discover the horseshoe crab eggs, which serve as an addition to the gulls' widely varied diet—a dead fish, for instance, or the remains of somebody's picnic. They'll even take the eggs and young of other birds.

When a gull finds a clam, it may fly high into the air and drop it to the rocks or hard-packed sand below. It does this again and again, until the shell of the unfortunate mollusk cracks from the impact. Cars passing along shore roads are sometimes pelted by these plummeting clams. White images of gulls are sometimes stenciled on road surfaces in hopes that the birds will refrain from dropping clams on their "relatives."

There are several kinds of gulls along the coasts of New England and Long Island. The most common is the herring gull, with white body and tail, gray mantle of wings and back, and black wingtips. It is about two feet long, from head to tail. Black-backed gulls, less common, have a much darker mantle and are larger— about thirty inches long. Both these birds have a reddish spot near the end of the lower beak.

RINGBILLED GULL   HERRING GULL   GREATER
                                                        BLACKBACKED
                                                            GULL

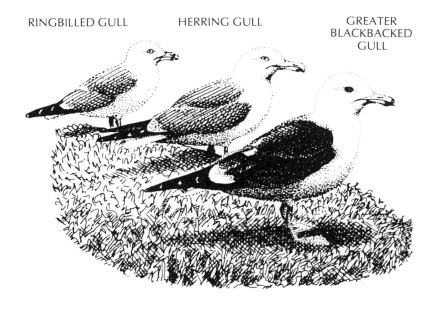

The laughing gull, named for its repetitious call, has a black head in summer (it's light gray in winter) and a dark gray mantle. It is about sixteen inches long. Gulls of most species take two or three years to mature; until then, the speckled youngsters are hard to tell apart as they fly about.

In winter the population may be increased by the presence of ring-billed gulls. These look much like herring gulls but are slightly smaller and have a black band near the tip of the beak. Ring-bills, incidentally, are often seen on inland lakes and rivers; flocks of them frequently follow farm implements in the fields, searching for insects and rodents stirred up by machinery.

The gulls' little cousins, the terns, commonly travel parallel to the beach over the water. They have light-colored bodies, black caps, and forked tails. They fly a few dozen feet above the water, beak pointed downward, looking for fish. Terns often hover a few seconds, then plunge down after their prey.

LAUGHING GULL

TERNS

Long legs and long bills characterize the shorebirds known as sandpipers. The several sandpiper species are hard to tell apart and are mostly brownish in color. They fly from tidal marsh to sand bar, usually in flocks that bank and turn in perfect formation.

One sandpiper that seems perfectly tuned to the ceaseless rhythm of the waves is the light-colored, active little sprinter known as the sanderling. Found on coasts throughout the world—and sometimes on freshwater lakeshores as well—these sparrow-size sandpipers race up the beach just ahead of a wave. When the water comes to a stop, they immediately turn and follow it back. As they go, they plunge their little black beaks repeatedly into the sand after worms and crustaceans.

SANDERLING

Besides affording a view of the antics of living creatures, a walk on a sandy beach provides the constant suspense that something new may be tossed up by the sea. Each turn of the tide may reveal a relic of the deep, such as the strings of papery discs that are the egg cases of the channeled whelk.

The shell of this big snail is also often found on the beach, and it seems to echo the roaring noise of the sea as you hold it to your ear. One youngster demonstrated the ocean sound of a large shell to her friend. The second girl listened in wonder a few minutes, then handed it back. "How often does it need batteries?" she asked.

You may also find the "sea collars" formed by the moon snail or the snail's empty shell itself. The shell is almost spherical (hence the lunar name) and sometimes as large as a ping-pong ball. The snail lays its eggs in a mucus band formed around its shell. Sand sticks to the mucus as the snail crawls away, leaving the "collar" behind.

The black "mermaid's purse," rectangular in shape with prong-like corners, is actually the egg case of the skate, a flattened relative of sharks. The eighteen-inch skate lives on the ocean bottom, swimming by the graceful, undulating motions of its wide pectoral fins. Its slender tail looks like that of its cousin the stingray, but the skate is harmless to people.

46

One of the most popular activities at the beach is collecting shells and other souvenirs of animals. Scores—indeed, thousands —of mollusk shells, some from as far away as the tropics, may wash ashore after a storm. Worn pebbles, beautiful when wet, catch your attention. Claws and shells of lobsters and crabs, fish bones and scales, sharks' teeth—these can make any beach walk fascinating.

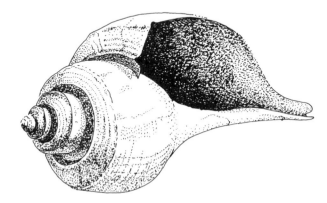

CHANNELED WHELK

MOONSNAIL AND EGG CASE

Jellyfish and comb jellies, stranded by waves or tide, attest to the amazing variety of life in the sea. Jellyfish, incidentally, usually travel along by opening and closing their cup-shaped bodies like umbrellas. Comb jellies, sometimes called sea walnuts or ctenophores, swim by the steady beating of rows of little paddles or combs. Ctenophores do not sting, but a true jellyfish is to be treated with respect. A distant tropical relative, the Portuguese man-of-war, has been known to paralyze human swimmers who have contacted its long tentacles in the water.

MOON JELLY

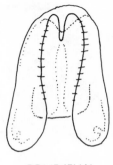
COMB JELLY

Many creatures of the sandy shore can also be found among the rocks or on the mud flats. Tides and waves act as great mixers, and the inhabitants of the oceans do not read the books that tell where they are supposed to be found. Peg and I went to view an unfortunate (and very dead) sixty-five-foot finback whale that had beached itself in Maine, for instance, and a tropical barracuda was recently washed ashore on Long Island.

Not long ago I discovered a colony of oysters on a rocky Cape Cod jetty. I asked a fisheries warden about the pollution dangers of eating oysters from the area. "No pollution to worry about around there," he answered. "But then, no oysters either." So along with Lisa Prescott and her artist husband, Reed—whose pictures grace these pages—Peg and I had a wonderful stew that evening. It was enriched with about two dozen pollution-free (and supposedly nonexistent) oysters.

CHAPTER 6

Tide-Pool Worlds

With thousands of kinds of life casting their young upon the waters in the form of eggs and larvae and miniatures of themselves, the ocean contains millions of marine gardens just waiting to happen. This is what helps make a tide pool so interesting.

Any hollow or depression, big or little, can become a fascinating place if it's touched by the tide. You never know what you'll find there. Each tide advances, then leaves behind the latest flotilla of little drifters in their new-washed tide-pool aquarium. Some of them depart on the next ebb and flow, while others settle into their new surroundings in welcome freedom from hungry enemies and the competition of their own kind.

Tide pools come in many shapes and sizes. They may be temporary—your footprint in the wet sand, for instance—or they may literally be carved in stone, where a cleft between rocks shelters a miniature inland sea. They may be mere inch-deep ripple marks on a mud or sand flat, or they may be mile-long troughs between an offshore bar and the mainland. Any of these will reward you if you give it more than a passing glance.

Consider your watery footprint. The muddy sand on which you are walking is alive with crawling, gliding, swimming creatures, many of whom will venture out into the water when the tide is full. When you create that little hollow, it is as if the "tide" has returned. Life resumes its pace as marine worms stretch out, as a few little crustaceans swim about, and as other assorted small opportunists explore the confines of their new size 10½-D universe.

If you want to join them, so to speak, take leave of your dignity for a while. Cast decorum to one side and get down on all fours in the sand or on the rocks—or in the mud, for that matter. As you contemplate the scene before you even without a magnifying glass, you'll begin to realize just how vibrant the sea is with living creatures. It has been said that if life in freshwater has the density of a morning mist, ocean life has the density of a thick pea soup.

Usually the more permanent the tide pool, the more extensive and mixed its population. Examine a quiet basin between the tumbled chunks of a New Hampshire breakwater, for instance. You may find the rocks there encrusted with thousands of barnacles and carpeted with great patches of tiny mussels. Scores of periwinkle snails and oyster drills poke along. You may discover a slow-moving starfish, a few of its sea-urchin cousins, and a dozen or more tiny crabs under a blanket of rockweed—plus a lively eel that almost upsets you as it thrashes its way out of your alien presence.

Some of the grandest tide pools are found in the stretch of more than fifty miles along each shore of Cape Cod. So gradual is the slope from the land to the depths along this peninsula that only a couple of feet of tidal fall uncovers a "flat" hundreds of yards wide. When the tide is at its lowest, the strip of exposed sea floor may be more than a mile wide—and filled with tide pools.

Much of this saturated sandy plain is dotted with pits and depressions and tiny lagoons. Small rivulets trace their paths out to the distant sea, some from freshwater brooks, others from the sand itself as it drains. Cape Cod's mixture of wet and dry, salt water and fresh, sandy bottom and scattered rocks, has a variety scarcely found anywhere else along our coast.

One afternoon, Peg and I stood looking at a water-filled drag mark in the sand at low tide. The mark had been made by a boat left behind as the water retreated, leaving a tide pool. All at once, this sun-dappled sluiceway burst into violent agitation as scores of little sand perch dashed back and forth. The dark markings on these fishes' bodies broke up their outlines so effectively that we could not actually see an individual one. Yet there they were, two-inch racers, disappearing in plain sight, a hundred of them—or was it only ten?

A horseshoe crab leaves a furrow as it plows through the top layer of wet sand. Other tide-pool depressions hold toad crabs, rock shrimp, sand eels, and active little razor clams that can upend and disappear into the sand in five seconds.

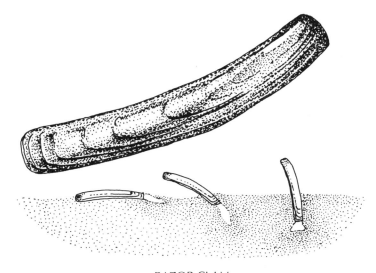

RAZOR CLAM

Any little watery basin can hold a moon snail, half buried in the sand. It pokes along in apparent innocence until some scent or motion betrays the presence of a sand worm or other prey. Then the moon snail's manner changes ominously. Its flexible body stretches out into a probing arm that feels around like a groping hand until it grips its prey. In only a few seconds the victim is smothered in a deadly blanket of flesh. The moon snail's rasping tongue begins its works, and soon the deed is done.

The abundance of life in tide pools is by no means lost on the flocks of water birds, schools of fish, and crowds of people who visit here. "The Cape," as it's often called, is a favorite with birders at all seasons. Anglers take to boats or to the pounding surf every month of the year.

Once when our son Roger and his wife Nancy were surf fishing near the Cape Cod Canal, they saw a commotion in the water. Hundreds of feeding bluefish were ravaging some smaller species, chopping them into bits. Gulls wheeled and screamed above the carnage, diving to snatch pieces of the unfortunate little fish. One gull landed on the water for a moment—and instantly was dragged from sight.

Tidal pools seem less fearsome when they lie quietly in the sun. Much of the life-and-death drama of the food chain takes place in silence, or at least it is inaudible to human hearing.

Winter tide pools are rewarding to visit; the winter ocean currents can carry little seafarers quite different from those in summer. But often in winter there's nobody to share the thrill of discovery. I once found a lively little squid among the wave-washed rocks near New London. The squid was the size of a hot dog, and it was vainly trying to hide under a bit of seaweed. It turned from pink to white to a mottled brown as it struggled. But there was not a soul for miles, it seemed—except the squid and me.

SQUID

If you are tempted to explore the world of the tide pool, I'd suggest you wear an old pair of sneakers or shoes with nonskid soles, even in summer. You might especially consider such footwear if you're squeamish about mud and sand oozing up around your toes. Besides, sneakers may preserve your equilibrium in case you happen to step on Something That Moved. Surefooted protection is also good if you're investigating rocky tide pools. No matter how careful you are, a single slip on barnacle-encrusted stones can result in a nasty scrape.

Considering our modern world, you could get cut on a fragment of glass or metal as well. I'd rather not have to mention that peril, but litter is there, and it's not about to go away. One scuba-diving friend came upon an old automobile tire marked "inflate to 70 pounds" in thirty feet of water. That pressure has seldom been used in tires for sixty years or more, showing that litter is scarcely a problem only of today.

Tidepool crabs, starfish, and sea worms may seem quite at home in the pools, but they have little control over how they get there. As newly hatched larvae floating on the surface, they simply drift on ocean currents. So do baby oysters, barnacles, sea anemones, and many other creatures. Only a few of these little adventurers ever arrive at a welcoming pool along the shore. The rest, in their millions, never find a home.

Seaweeds, too, often become tidepool residents by chance. Broken off in a storm, a portion of the weed may be deposited hundreds of miles from the parent plant. Attached to the seaweed may be a few slipper shells, barnacles, and a sea anemone. There they remain, setting up shop in their new surroundings, while every high water obligingly brings in a new crop to feed them.

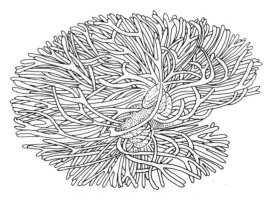

SEAWEED AND SHELLS

Perhaps a word is in order about tides themselves. As is well known, they're caused when the water creeps up the beach and back in response to the pull of the moon. Since the moon rises about fifty minutes later each day, there is a corresponding lag in the tides.

But less known is the effect of the sun on tides. The sun's pull is weaker because it is so far away. About twice a month the sun and moon are more or less in line with each other, and the tides attain their greatest height. These spring tides, as they are called, occur at full moon and new moon each month.

When the moon is high in the sky and the sun is on the horizon, the effects of the two tend to cancel each other out and there's a weaker or neap tide. Thus, when you're in Buffalo, say, a glance at the sun and moon can tell you the relative strength of the tides they're having back in Boston.

Changing tides may have a marked effect on the activities of sea creatures. Some kinds of marine worms, lobsters, and sand dollars—to name but a few—are most active when the tide is rising. So are a number of fish.

At the mouth of a river on the Connecticut shore of Long Island Sound, my father was once joyously overwhelmed when a school of pollack on an incoming tide attacked his lure. No sooner had he released one fish than he had another, again and again. Then the tide changed—and not a pollack could be induced to bite, even though the great school was still swirling right below his pole.

Considering this constant flow of water and its varied offerings, I made a list of the population in a single tide pool about the size of a card table. The pool, near Riverhead, Long Island, typified those found along the northeastern coast. Doubtless I missed many living things, but the tally included brown rockweed and its distant green relative, mermaid's hair; sea lettuce; strips of kelp; two kinds of barnacles; a sea cucumber; a starfish; several sea anemones; three species of fish, including silverside minnows and a tiny flounder; several dozen periwinkles; dog whelks; speckled flatworms; rock crabs; mussels; encrusting sponges—and one dead jellyfish.

A sandy pool near Misquamicut, Rhode Island, sheltered eel-grass and its vertically swimming companion, the pipefish; a few hermit crabs in their commandeered snail shells; the ever-present whelks and winkles; two sand dollars the size of pennies (the adults usually have the size, shape, and fragility of cookies). All doubtless breathed a collective gurgle of relief when I picked a carnivorous moon snail from their midst and tossed it out into deeper water.

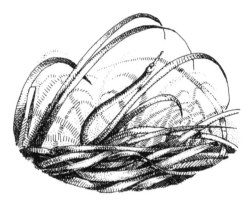

PIPEFISH AND EELGRASS

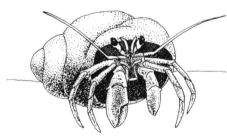

HERMIT CRAB

SAND DOLLAR

There is one group of living things you'll seldom find in any tide pool, although this great mass of creatures is present in abundance almost everywhere else on land, in the air, and in freshwater: insects. Few insects live around salt water. There are saltwater mosquitoes, true, but their home is really in brackish swamps. A few beetles and flies live where the salt is tempered by freshwater, but that's about as far as insects go.

Only a few insect species attempt to take any kind of ocean trip. One such voyager is the water strider, a cousin of those familiar skaters that dimple the surfaces of almost every inland pond and stream. Indeed, the strider has been found many miles at sea.

Another insect, much smaller but often numbering in the tens of thousands, is the tiny springtail or water hopper. The springtail does not go below the water, but its legions may blanket the surface so the pool beneath is hidden from view. Some of them are red and some are white, but most are an ashy gray and not much larger than a grain of sugar.

Beyond these two, however, you'll probably never see an ocean-going insect. All the bees, gnats, and dragonflies you encounter—even the pesky biting greenhead fly—got their start somewhere inland. If you find an insect crawling groggily on a mud flat or walking bedraggled on a sandy beach, it's probably there because retreating waves left it there.

And, doubtless, that little insect Jonah will be just as happy if the waves continue to stay away.

GREENHEAD FLY

CHAPTER 7

Flotsam and Jetsam

One of the joys of visiting the seashore is the possibility of seeing the unexpected. You can walk the edge of the sea every day, but it'll never be quite the same.

When I was a boy, I often scouted the beaches at Hammonasset in Connecticut and Watch Hill in Rhode Island in hopes of finding ambergris. This is the pungent material tossed up by sick sperm whales and is highly valued in the perfume industry. I had been told that if I found a piece even the size of a baseball, my fortune would be made.

Nary a whiff of ambergris ever came to my attention. Today, there are so few sperm whales in the oceans that little ambergris is likely to be found on beaches. But the hours and miles I walked along the shore brought me the realization that almost anything that does drift in the sea can eventually find its way to land.

So varied and fleeting is the daily crop brought by the tide that even the National Park service sometimes posts an exception to its own rule of "leave nothing but footprints; take nothing but a picture." The myriad seashells and sticks and dried weeds and dead fish and sand and stones all get sorted and rearranged daily. There is no practical way to save them.

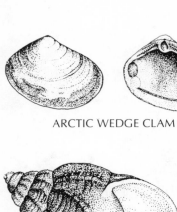

ARCTIC WEDGE CLAM

CROSSHATCHED LUCINE

PERIWINKLE

GREENLAND
TOP SHELL

COMMON NORTHERN WHELK

TURBONILLE

TELLIN

DOVE SHELL

ATLANTIC PLATE LIMPET

BAY SCALLOP

N.E. BASKET WHELK

WENTLETRAP

GREAT PIDDOCK

FILE YOLDIA

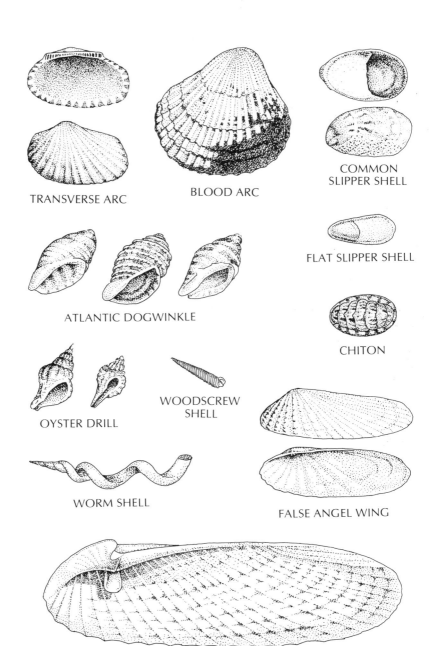

TRANSVERSE ARC

BLOOD ARC

COMMON
SLIPPER SHELL

ATLANTIC DOGWINKLE

FLAT SLIPPER SHELL

CHITON

OYSTER DRILL

WOODSCREW
SHELL

WORM SHELL

FALSE ANGEL WING

ANGEL WING

Might as well pick up that pretty pebble or scallop shell—both of them will be buried or washed away on the next tide anyway. Sometimes they're accompanied by hundreds of others just like themselves. A gravel bar may exhibit thousands of stones almost exactly the same size, for instance, or a few dozen square feet of shoreline may consist entirely of oyster shells.

The laws of fluid dynamics explain the sifting and sorting, but when you find hundreds of jingle shells, for example, in a patch ten yards wide—and nowhere else on the whole beach—you care little about how the currents brought them there. Those translucent wafer-thin yellow discs from unseen little clams still sound like elfin bells when you shake them together in your hand.

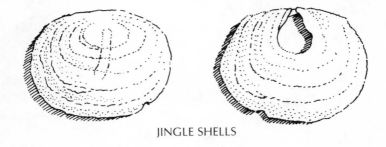

JINGLE SHELLS

You feel you've accomplished something when you find a perfect arc shell with both halves still joined, there at the edge of the waves. You brave the swash of the breakers to rescue a ribbon of kelp and haul it ashore. You examine the barnacles and slipper shells and bryozoans and other crusty creatures along that leathery brown alga's ten-foot length. You consider the blue mussel shell still gripped by the kelp's rootlike holdfast; then you consign the whole works to the briny once more.

Flotsam and jetsam, these orphans of the sea are called. And seldom are they more evident than in the tangles of debris tossed up and abandoned in rows on the beach. The highest row has been there the longest—deposited, perhaps, by a storm or by the spring tide of a week or two ago—while lower rows have arrived more recently.

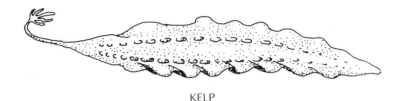

KELP

Once, at Hampton Beach, New Hampshire, Peg and I were looking for unusual shells, rocks, and small crustaceans in the rows of tidal debris to help populate our marine aquarium. As we overturned chunks of dried seaweed and driftwood, three children joined us. Soon their parents came along. Our group was then enlarged by several others. Ultimately, we'd have needed a couple of buckets to hold all they found and dutifully brought to us!

It would be pointless to try to list what the sea may provide you on your next visit. The collection Peg and I have amassed would bear little relation to yours. Just to name a few things, however: we've found several colorful lobster-pot buoys; pieces of rope, both long and short; shells and calico rocks by the hundreds of pounds; an extinct fishpole and reel; a thirty-inch swordfish sword; several dozen sharks' teeth; a life preserver labeled "Mame"; an entire crate of ocean-marinated oranges; two dolphin skeletons; a dead baby whale; and a faded—but still negotiable—dollar bill. (That bill, by the way, was the first time I've known a beachcomber to get a tip.)

Two scourges have plagued our natural world during the last few years: plastic six-pack ring holders and tangles of fishline. I recall a photograph of a young seal that was slowly strangled by the confining collar of a six-pack holder around its neck. Many a gull, heron, or other bird has floundered and died in the clutches of a mess of discarded fishline. On one Florida beach we watched helplessly as a pelican half-swam and half-flew out beyond the waves, its wing bound to its beak by a large fishing plug and line.

But few things in this world are all bad or all good, even the items we toss away. It is hard to imagine what could be good about fragments of broken glass, but let the waves tumble the pieces about in the sand for a few weeks, and the edges become harmlessly dull while the surface is eroded to an attractive frosty white. Craft shops along our coasts now feature these tumbled glass items as souvenirs. One shop near Providence sells night lights, bracelets, necklaces, and stained-glass panels fashioned from "tidal jewels," as their designer calls them. The cost of the colored materials: zero.

In several places off the Atlantic and Pacific coasts, experiments have been conducted with old automobile tires. They are chained together, weighted, and sunk to the bottom; once they have settled, they provide hiding places and potential nurseries for marine life. Weeds and sea animals attach to them, adding to the available food and shelter. Soon the larger species move in—and "the fishing is better on the junk pile," as one charter boat captain told me.

Many such "junk piles" have inadvertently been created by cargo washed overboard from storm-battered freighters, by sunken ships, and by submarines depth-bombed in two world wars. More than two thousand such wrecks litter the East Coast from North Carolina's Outer Banks—the "Graveyard of the Atlantic"—to Labrador. Any storm or any change in the great off-shore currents such as the Gulf Stream may release a bit of deep-sea treasure and start it on its voyage shoreward.

One battered hulk lies just off the west coast of Wellfleet, near the tip of Cape Cod. This ship was used for target practice during World War II and now rests peacefully on a sand bar. Occasionally, a chunk of wood or metal is freed by corrosion and is washed ashore. We once found a section of a ship's bell in its vicinity. Perhaps it was a souvenir from the beleaguered craft, perhaps not—but it's fun to speculate.

If you *do* feel inclined to pick up souvenirs along the sand, be sure to take along a sturdy bag or sack. In fact, take more than one—that stone doorstep is scarcely the best company for a delicate angel-wing shell. Also, in the unlikely event that there's only one bag's worth of natural material to collect, you'll still have a handy litter bag.

And if you have two containers, you can share your load with a friend who comes along only for the walk—but who might be persuaded to help you with your burden. Perhaps your friend will even carry the doorstop.

When you find a rock or shell or old brass hinge for your shelf or coffee table, consider how it will look when it's dry and away from the shore before you put it in your bag. Part of the charm of a souvenir is the mood, the frame of mind that goes along with it. A sparkling piece of granite, wet with the sea water on a gorgeous summer afternoon, may look pretty dull by the time you get it home.

Some people keep their shells and rocks in water in a glass jar. Others put a transparent coat of varnish on them to help retain their original gloss and color. Photographers may take pictures of their souvenirs and mount the enlargements on the wall.

None of these, of course, quite recaptures the thrill of first discovery. Peg and I have found this out over the years. Now we reluctantly pass up that pretty pink shell, that gleaming black rock. We know they're at their best when being tossed and swirled by the waves as a vital piece in the mosaic of the seashore—a tableau that can never be recaptured at home.

Yet many items do make wonderful take-home articles. Consider driftwood, for instance. Like snowflakes, probably no two pieces are the same. They can be fine additions to table decorations and have been used to make everything from chairs to floor lamps. Even when put to no real use, they can stir the imagination—just as they did when you picked them up.

With a chunk of driftwood, you usually get shape, color, and texture that are unique. The abrasive action of wind, wave, and sand have accented the grain of the wood, and the sun has bleached the color. Borers have sculpted a maze of tunnels. Since driftwood is often the remains of a stump or a tree that has fallen into a river and been washed to sea, weird shapes of the roots may be there as well.

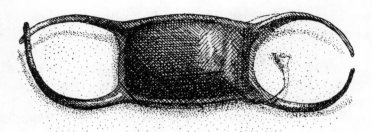

MERMAID'S PURSE
(see page 46)

Look for these and other ocean castaways right after a storm, if you get the chance. Not only does the storm toss floating debris up on the beach, but the pounding surf may uncover long-hidden objects as well. A few large links of chain were once exposed by a gale and noticed by a youngster; they led to the discovery of the anchor of a Civil War ship. The anchor now rests on its own special mount in Chincoteague, Virginia.

Of course, some storms dislodge objects that were intended to stay put. At Phippsburg, Maine, great chunks of rock, truck bodies, and whole automobiles were chained together in an effort to halt the march of the sea toward people's cottages and old homes. It was a losing battle—the waves driven by a howling gale smashed, ripped, and nearly obliterated the whole affair.

Several buildings, however, were saved. They were jacked up and moved back a few hundred feet. In fact, they may be secure now precisely because nature performs what human beings cannot. Between the houses and the ocean a strip of common beach grass has established itself. The wiry stems and interlaced roots of that rugged plant form a huge resilient mat—almost a welcome mat—inviting the sea to come ashore and rest awhile.

CHAPTER 8

Whale Watch

As recently as a generation ago, if you wanted to see a whale, chances were you'd have to visit a large oceanarium or book passage on an ocean liner. Maybe you'd even have to go for a trip on a whaling vessel.

Today, things are easier. For about fifteen dollars, more or less, you can board an excursion boat, position yourself at the vessel's rail, and see a living whale within an hour—almost guaranteed. Boats leave from points along both coasts of the United States, including Hawaii—and from Canadian and Mexican ports as well. More than nine times out of ten, their search is amply rewarded.

The modern "whaling" vessels, such as ones we've taken from Newburyport, Massachusetts, from New Hampshire's Rye Harbor, and from Cape Cod's Provincetown, are well equipped for the task. The several dozen passengers (some boats can carry a hundred or more) have plenty of space on the decks—or inside in case it rains. There are rest rooms (the "head," in nautical parlance) and, of course, a snack bar.

If you go on such an ocean voyage, I'd suggest you find a boat with a naturalist on board who will give you an introduction to the great creatures beforehand. You'll learn there are two main groups of them.

The first group consists of the toothed whales, such as the sperm whale of *Moby Dick* fame, and his frisky little cousins, the dolphins and porpoises. Group two contains the baleen whales, whose mouthparts include a comblike fringe or baleen for straining small food organisms from the water.

The boat's naturalist will most likely have a sample of this baleen (also called whalebone) for you to handle and examine. Chances are you'll marvel that such a seive supplies as much as a ton of small fish, sand eels, and shrimp-size crustaceans (called krill) every day of a large whale's life.

Even if you don't spot a single whale—an extremely unlikely turn of events—there is still plenty to see. Our most recent trip, for instance, was enlivened by the antics of an oceanic bird known as the Manx shearwater, which dived and wheeled and almost cut the waves with a wingtip (hence its name). Dubbed "Mad Manx" by the crew and passengers, the shearwater flew beneath the swift boat's projecting prow, then zoomed into the air and back to the surface again.

We had visits from petrels, too—ocean birds the size of a robin that have a habit of flying with their feet occasionally pattering on the surface, which has given them their name. "Petrel," it seems, means "little Peter," in allusion to the disciple who walked on the water. Once a single ocean sunfish, or mola mola, as big as a card table, lay flat on the surface and waved a companionable fin at us as we went by. The week before our visit, the boat nearly rammed a basking shark the size of a hippopotamus that, like the baleen whales, was leisurely feeding on tiny organisms strained from the water.

No two whale trips are alike. Even the same boat taking the same trip in the afternoon over the same water that it took in the morning may encounter new experiences. On one early trip, we were entertained by nearly a hundred white-sided dolphins, cavorting and leaping clear of the water and easily keeping pace with our boat as it headed for the whale grounds at full speed. The afternoon cruise produced not a single dolphin, but the passengers were drenched as an exuberant humpback whale leaped clear of the water just a few feet from the boat.

Most of the vessels are in radio contact with each other. Thus, as a mother humpback and her baby (if you can call a ten-ton youngster a baby) loafed on the surface, they entertained four boatloads of passengers in succession. Even without radios, the vessels observe each other's actions, thereby boosting the success rate for all.

For centuries, towns like Mystic, New Bedford, and Provincetown were the centers of much of American whaling. From these and other ports, men went to sea in pursuit of the peaceful giants who lazed through the fertile waters of the Gulf of Maine from Newfoundland to New York and beyond.

There was a good reason for the whales to gather off those coasts. The bottom of the ocean is seldom a great, smooth underwater plain; it's scalloped and gouged by ditches and chasms. Folds and ridges create barriers to the flow of ocean currents such as the Gulf Stream, causing massive upwellings of water from the deeps. These upwellings bring with them the fertility from the bottom, rich with minerals and recycled nutrients from sea creatures of long ago. In such areas, the great whales feed on the abundant marine life.

Two of the most productive of these regions are the Georges Banks and the Stellwagen Banks, just a few miles off our New England coast. On many days you can see a watery pathway, different in color and smoother in appearance, running through the choppy waves surrounding it. This pathway is visible evidence of the constant tilling of this undersea garden.

Several species of whales make their seasonal home in these waters. On our various trips we've seen swift little minke whales, long and graceful finbacks, acrobatic humpbacks, and on only two occasions, the North Atlantic right whale. The right whale, the rarest and most endangered of all whales, received its name because it was the "right" whale to kill. When dead, it remains at the surface instead of needing floats to keep it from sinking.

Your first glimpse of a whale is likely to be a puff of mist that rises for a moment above the waves. This, the creature's exhaled breath, tends to turn to fog when it hits the cool sea air, just as your breath does on a cold day. Sometimes the whale "blows" just before breaking the surface, carrying sea water into the air as well.

Usually the sighting of the misty plume is followed by a glimpse of a long dark shape; then (depending on the species) you may see the arched hump of a back and the brief appearance of a dorsal fin. If you're close enough you'll hear an explosive burst of air, followed by a cavernous intake as the whale gulps a new breath. Then, for another few minutes or for as much as a quarter hour, silence.

Peg and I have slept along the shores of Mexico's Baja Peninsula, where California gray whales bear their young. Beyond the gentle ripples lapping the shore of Scammon's lagoon, we could hear a steady rumble as of the surf, out there in the darkness. It wasn't surf, however, but the sound of fifty or more whales filling their great lungs half a mile away.

Often you'll encounter females with young. The two may rise to the surface almost together: the ten-foot misty "spout" is accompanied by a smaller puff only half as high.

Of course, even a baby whale is impressive: it is about fifteen feet long and weighs several tons at birth, depending on the species. While most mammals are born head first, the whale youngster's tail is the first to emerge—otherwise it might drown before it could get that first gasp of air. It may be nudged to the surface by solicitous relatives, swimming close by the new mother.

Along almost any coast where whales are found, large boats and small are there to help you visit them. In many places the boats operate under restrictions: it is against the law to chase or harass whales, even with good intentions, such as seeking to take a closeup picture or merely to get a better view.

From the times we have drifted among these creatures in both the Atlantic and Pacific oceans, Peg and I feel there's no such thing as sneaking up on a whale. Using their eyes and their fine sense of hearing, they are keenly aware of the watery world around them. I believe one of the reasons the whalers were so successful is that their quarry did not suspect those little boats meant any harm. So the gray whales probably regarded the whale hunter for whom Scammon's lagoon in Mexico is named.

The modern New England "whaler" takes you to a more peaceful encounter. Not only is it hoped you'll have one of the unforgettable times of your life, but many whale-watch boats take careful notes on each cruise, gaining valuable data while these fascinating creatures remain in existence.

Partly for this purpose, many of these boats have a naturalist aboard. Individual whales have marks or patterns on their bodies by which they can be identified. The "flukes," or broad tail, of the humpback whale, for instance, can carry a black-white pattern on the underside that is as distinctive as a fingerprint. "There's Ruby," your naturalist guide may say after a glance at the tail pattern, "back from the Caribbean with this year's baby."

The humpback is an individual in many ways. Big as a bus, its seemingly oversized white flippers are the aquatic version of the forearms of its landlubber ancestors. It is one of the most vocal of whales, with a complex assortment of squeals, clicks, groans, and whistles. And it sometimes traps its food by the use of bubbles.

In this "bubble feeding," one or more whales go beneath a school of small fish or plankton. The whales release streams of bubbles that surround or come up through the school, creating a "wall" in the water. The fishes, confused by the bubbles, mill around in a circle. Up through them comes the humpback, and its capacious mouth scoops up the prey. Driving with those mighty flukes, it lunges partway out of the sea, water streaming through the baleen plates, while the wriggling captives go down by the bushel.

Gulls, wheeling above the melee, dive for the fish that escape. We've seen them fly right through that great open mouth, and more than once an unfortunate bird has become part of the humpback's meal.

One of the most spectacular displays in the ocean is the "breach," or leap, of a humpback. Up from the depths comes the whale, exploding from the water in a fountain of spray. White flippers and underbelly gleam for a moment as fifty tons of whale are suspended, sometimes completely clear of the water. Then, with a thunderous crash, it falls back into the sea. One September

HUMPBACK WHALE

day, on a boat out of Provincetown, we watched as a whale breached time after time—a dozen leaps or more.

No one is sure just why whales breach like this. Perhaps it's exuberance, perhaps it's a way to impress the ladies (males do this more frequently), or possibly it's to dislodge external parasites. "Then, too," the naturalist on the boat told me, "we may not have the answer at all."

Indeed, there may be no answer. After all, you and I can scarcely explain our own behavior, sometimes.

A quieter but equally impressive display of the power of a large whale is the whale's "footprint." Usually, as a whale "sounds," or turns sharply downward for a deep dive, it raises its tail flukes above the water for a moment. Then, to drive that massive body into the depths, it gives a mighty thrust with its tail. This produces the footprint—a circular boil in the water, sometimes twenty feet or more in diameter, that remains for several minutes, even in a heavy sea.

Time was that whales numbered in the hundreds of thousands. The demand for their meat, whalebone (baleen), and oil brought their populations down to alarmingly low levels. The North

Atlantic right whale, for instance, may number only three hundred individuals in the entire world instead of the tens of thousands that once existed.

An enlightened attitude toward these great creatures has brought a new awareness of the peril that faces them. In addition, there are modern alternatives to their earlier uses for dog food, cosmetics, oil, and photographic film. Most whaling countries have declared a moratorium on the commercial taking of the large species, despite understandable resistance from the people whose livelihood depended on them. (Whales are still taken for "research" in an effort to circumvent this international agreement.)

The Center for Coastal Studies (CCS) in Provincetown has a wealth of information on the lives of thousands of whales—many of which are known as individuals. Each is eagerly looked for from one year to the next. The Center's programs of education and research have made countless friends since its beginning in 1975.

Thanks to the work done by CCS and the marine biologists of many universities and private foundations, the beleaguered sea mammals have a new lease on life. If you can, take a whale-watch boat sometime from April to October and see for yourself. Then, perhaps, you'll understand when marine biologists tell you that, at last, a living whale is worth more than a dead one.

And there they are—the whales and whelks and seaweeds and sand dunes of our New England coast. These few pages with their handful of illustrations can scarcely serve even as an introduction to it all.

The Maine coast alone, we are told, would stretch across our continent if all the shores, islands, and inlets were laid end to end. We are also told that the shorelines of the other New England states (except landlubber Vermont) would bring us about half way back. To explore all of this—dune and rock and tidepool—would take a lifetime. With the changeability of our restless sea, in fact, we'd be at it forever.

All we can hope is that we've whetted your appetite for the wonders that await you, so to speak, with every wave. Perhaps we can put it all in perspective by quoting the renowned biologist Louis Agassiz. Once he was asked how he had occupied himself the previous summer.

"I spent it traveling," he answered.

"Oh? And where did you go?"

"Where did I go" the great naturalist repeated. "Well—I went halfway across my back yard."

THE END

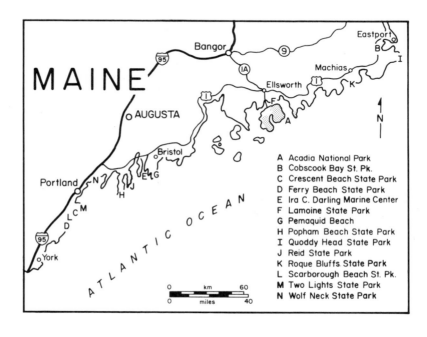

A Acadia National Park
B Cobscook Bay St. Pk.
C Crescent Beach State Park
D Ferry Beach State Park
E Ira C. Darling Marine Center
F Lamoine State Park
G Pemaquid Beach
H Popham Beach State Park
I Quoddy Head State Park
J Reid State Park
K Roque Bluffs State Park
L Scarborough Beach St. Pk.
M Two Lights State Park
N Wolf Neck State Park

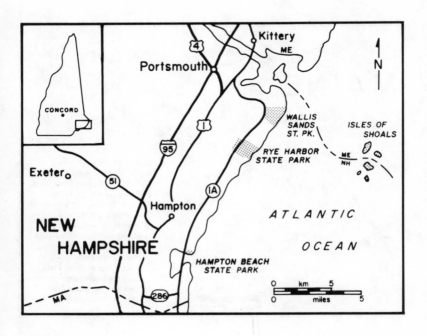

CONCORD

Kittery
ME

Portsmouth

4

1

95

WALLIS
SANDS
ST. PK.

ISLES OF
SHOALS

RYE HARBOR
STATE PARK

ME
NH

Exeter

51

1A

ATLANTIC

Hampton

NEW
HAMPSHIRE

OCEAN

HAMPTON BEACH
STATE PARK

MA

286

km   5

miles   5

N

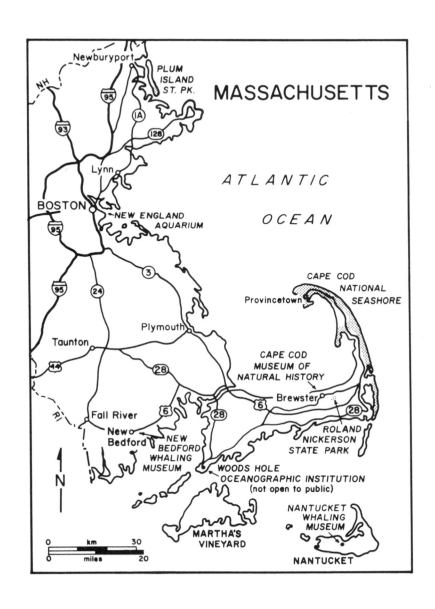

MASSACHUSETTS

ATLANTIC

OCEAN

Newburyport

PLUM
ISLAND
ST. PK.

NH

95

1A

128

93

Lynn

BOSTON

NEW ENGLAND
AQUARIUM

95

3

95

24

Plymouth

Taunton

44

28

CAPE COD
NATIONAL
SEASHORE

Provincetown

CAPE COD
MUSEUM OF
NATURAL HISTORY

Brewster

6

28

6

28

Fall River

RI

New
Bedford

NEW
BEDFORD
WHALING
MUSEUM

ROLAND
NICKERSON
STATE PARK

WOODS HOLE
OCEANOGRAPHIC INSTITUTION
(not open to public)

N

NANTUCKET
WHALING
MUSEUM

MARTHA'S
VINEYARD

NANTUCKET

| 0 | km | 30 |
| 0 | miles | 20 |

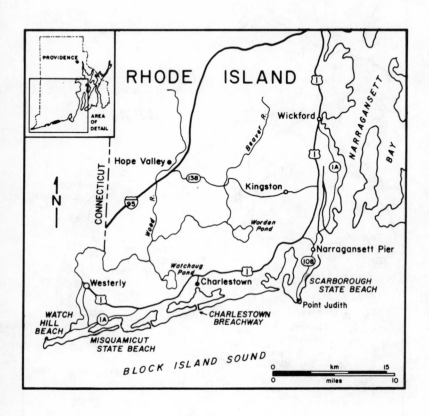

RHODE ISLAND

PROVIDENCE

AREA OF DETAIL

N

CONNECTICUT

Hope Valley

95

138

Wood R.

Beaver R.

Wickford

NARRAGANSETT

BAY

1A

Kingston

Worden Pond

Narragansett Pier

108

SCARBOROUGH STATE BEACH

Watchaug Pond

Charlestown

Westerly

CHARLESTOWN BREACHWAY

Point Judith

WATCH HILL BEACH

1A

MISQUAMICUT STATE BEACH

BLOCK ISLAND SOUND

km

0   15

miles

0   10

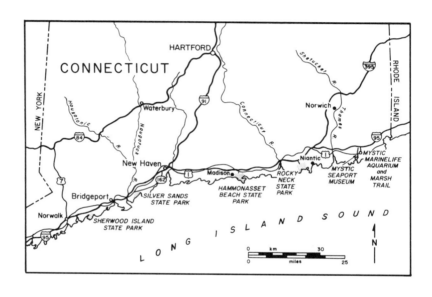

Index

Crab
   blue, 22
   calico, see Crab, lady
   fiddler, 22; *illus. 22*
   hermit, 55; *illus. 55*
   horseshoe, 41, 51; *illus. 42*
   king, 41
   lady, 40; *illus. 41*
   mole, see Hippa
   spider, 41; *illus. 42*
   rock, 31
Ctenophore, see Comb jelly
Cucumber, sea, 32, 54; *illus. 33*

Damselfly, 14; *illus. 14*
Diatoms, 23
Dogwinkle, Atlantic, *illus. 59*
Dolphins, 61, 66
Dove, mourning, 11; *illus. 12*
Dragonfly, 14
Driftwood, 63
Drill, 30
   oyster, 50; *illus. 59*
Duck
   eider, 36
   scoter, 36
Dusty miller, 8; *illus. 8*

Eel, 30, 50
Eider, see Duck, eider

Featherweed, 30
Fern
   bracken, 4; *illus. 5*
   sweet, 4; *illus. 5*
Flea, sand, 40; *illus. 40*
Fly, greenhead, 56; *illus. 56*
Flycatcher, 12
Frogs, 16

Georges Banks, 67
Glass; 62
Glasswort, 20; *illus. 20*
Goldenrod, seashore, 19; *illus. 19*
Grackle, 13
Granite, 28, 63
Grape, wild, 9
Grass
   beach, 6, 64
   cord, 18; *illus. 18*
   eel, 55; *illus. 55*
   plume, 18
Gribble, 39
Gulf Stream, 67
Gull
   black-backed, 43; *illus. 43*
   herring, 43; *illus. 43*
   laughing, 44; *illus. 44*
   ring-billed, 44; *illus. 43*

Hammonasset State Park, Ct., 57
Harrier, northern, 12
Hawk, marsh, see Harrier,
   northern
Heron, great blue, 15, 26
Hippa, 39; *illus. 40*
Hydroid, 31

Isles of Shoals, 29
Isopod, 20; *illus. 21*
Ivy, poison, 9; *illus. 9*

Jellyfish, 23, 31, 48, 54; *illus. 48*

Kelp, 54, 60; *illus. 61*
Kestrel, 11; *illus. 11*
Krill, 66

Lettuce, sea, 30, 54

Limpet, 32
   Atlantic plate, *illus. 58*
Lobster, 54
Lucine, crosshatched, *illus. 58*

Maine, Gulf of, 67
Mallow
   marsh, 19; *illus. 19*
   rose, 19; *illus. 19*
Meadowlark, 13; *illus. 14*
"Mermaid's purse," 46; *illus. 64*
Mice, 10
Mosquitoes, 56
"Moss," Irish, 30
Muskrat, 15, 25; *illus. 25*
Mussel
   blue, 21, 30, 39, 50, 60;
      illus. 21
   gray-ribbed, 21; *illus. 21*
Mystic, Ct., 67

Nemertine, see Worm, ribbon
New Bedford, Ma., 67
Newburyport, Ma., 65

Opossum, 10; *illus. 10*
Osprey, 26; *illus. 26*
Otter, 26
Outer Banks, N.C., 62
Oyster, 33, 39, 48, 53, 60; *illus. 34*

Pea, beach, 7; *illus. 7*
Periwinkle, 30, 50, 54; *illus. 21, 58*
Petrel, 66
Phippsburg, Me., 64
Phoebe, 12; *illus. 13*

Phragmites, see Grass, plume
Piddock, great, *illus. 58*
Pipefish, 55; *illus. 55*
Plankton, 23, 33
Plover, 8
   piping, 9; *illus. 9*
Plum, beach, 4; *illus. 6*
Pollack, 54
Popham Beach, Me., 8
Porpoises, 66
Portuguese man-o-war, 48
Potomac River, 34
Providence, R.I., 62
Provincetown, Ma., 65, 67
Puffin, Atlantic, 36; *illus. 36*

Quahog, 21; *illus. 21*

Rabbit, cottontail, 10
Raccoon, 10, 25
Reed, marsh, see Grass, plume
Riverhead, N.Y., 54
Rockweed, 29, 50, 54; *illus. 29*
Rose, 9, 10
Rush, seaside, 18
Rye Harbor, N.H., 65

Samphire, see Glasswort
Sand dollar, 54, 55; *illus. 55*
Sanderling, 45; *illus. 46*
Sandpiper, 8, 26, 35; *illus. 35*
Scallop, bay, *illus. 58*
Scoter, see Duck, scoter
Sea collar, 46; *illus. 47*
Sea lavender, 18; *illus. 19*
Seal, 61
   harbor, 37
Seaweed, 53; *illus. 53*